CHATGPT

CHATGPT

A Guide to Business Success

BILL VINCENT

RWG Publishing

CONTENTS

1 Introduction 1

2 Understanding ChatGPT 2

3 Implementing ChatGPT in Business 3

4 Enhancing Customer Experience 4

5 Leveraging ChatGPT for Sales 6

6 ChatGPT for Marketing Strategies 8

7 ChatGPT for Customer Support 10

8 Ensuring Data Privacy and Security 12

9 Training and Managing ChatGPT 14

10 Monitoring and Improving Performance 16

11 Integrating ChatGPT with Existing Systems 18

12 Scaling ChatGPT for Large Businesses 20

13 Overcoming Challenges and Limitations 22

14 Ethical Considerations with ChatGPT 24

15 Future Trends and Developments 26

16 Conclusion 28

CHAPTER 1

Introduction

Chat marketing is more than real, and it is directly responsible for revolutionizing digital marketing strategies. Big brands like Apple, Domino's Pizza, Burger King, and Amazon have already developed their own chat marketing strategies to expand their businesses. Through chat marketing, these brands communicate with their consumers personally, aiming to create and maintain a unique and close relationship. In addition, they show that their products have something that differentiates and adds value, while also including a great user experience. This guide is aimed at professionals who do not yet have a chat marketing strategy and want to start implementing tactics that leverage business. It is based on proven examples of companies that already work and engage their customers through chat marketing, an internationally known strategy as Chatbot.

Imagine a marketing model in which you can directly communicate one-on-one with your audience and learn what they need, what they like, and what brings them back — all in real-time. Simultaneously, this kind of marketing is seen as a time and money investment. Do you think this model is too good to be true?

CHAPTER 2

Understanding ChatGPT

We do not need to look very far to understand why AI never lived up to the utopian visions laid out for it in the 60s and 70s. The same year ELIZA was created, Stanford Research Institute (now SRI International) released "Shakey". Shakey was a general purpose mobile robot that could "see" its environment through sprites and navigate it as well. The physical and software problems that needed to be solved were diverse in ways that make modern engineers thankful for the technical infrastructures we have. Without easy access to cloud services, fragmented and non-interoperable data storage options, computing power and memory limited by the technology of the age, and even basic software development tools that have become standard in our day, development time and costs were enormous.

The term chatbot has been around since 1966. Later that year, a company claimed they had a program that could beat the Turing Test. Created by Joseph Weizenbaum at the MIT AI lab, ELIZA was a computer program using pattern matching and substitution methodology to simulate conversation. By 1973, there was even a philosophy symposium about "the epic of conversation between man and machine". The future of AI looked so bright, that now over three decades later we are still working to live up to the dreams of AI that were already present in the beginning of the digital age.

CHAPTER 3

Implementing ChatGPT in Business

This second part started with the concepts and business applications of conversational transformation, i.e., CT. In this first chapter, the different technical alternatives for CT (data-driven models like GPT-3, models refining rule-based ones like BERT, or hybrid ones like Meena and LaMDA) were explained. Then, these alternatives were presented based on block diagrams from the CT perspective. Finally, a large number of examples of different CT applications in the business context were studied.

In the previous section, the different CT approaches were explained, explaining them represented on block diagrams, and showing several examples of what could be achieved using CT. It explained their large possible benefits and business applications. The main aim of this second part of the book is to provide readers with the necessary knowledge and tools to prepare their companies or startups for the next era in communication, called AI language. This section therefore is organized as follows:

CHAPTER 4

Enhancing Customer Experience

As part of the CX strategy, companies invest in a good relationship with customers, use referral programs, streamline service and sales, and create the logo and other specific applications. By aligning the client's experiences with the company's strategic interests, customer experience professionals work inside the organization with cross-functional teams. At times, this could mean championing project initiatives with third-party providers. Corporate executives who have determined success criteria, approved budgets, and ensured that the resources required with project management support are equipped to accomplish and amplify CX initiatives. Your clients/customers or stakeholders will undoubtedly conclude whether the initiative is a waste, an episode that becomes a viral hit. And they will indicate whether or not it should be repeated.

Outstanding customer experience can only be achieved with a combination of great product results and high levels of customer satisfaction and loyalty. Since first contact with a client, the implementation of customer experience strategies, called CX, has become a concern for the economic sector. The benefits go far beyond good results, since they not only ensure customer satisfaction, but also keep them loyal to the brand throughout their life cycle. Therefore, the level of customers remains high throughout the customer journey: from attraction and maintenance to loyalty and referral. For this, companies must be concerned not only with the service or product offered, but also with the client's perception of the brand.

CHAPTER 5

Leveraging ChatGPT
for Sales

After the sales process has started, ChatGPT is used to schedule a demo and collect contact data if the prospect needs an agreement. Moreover, if another contact has posted a request because of its interest in the company's lead, you can use ChatGPT to schedule a demo if a connection is from outside the company, no matter what form of collaboration they're aiming for. This AI-driven approach is extremely efficient. It completes 28 tasks in 8 minutes, representing a 20% productivity increase. Farmer connects an automation to the CRM and archive, they can kick back and let the ChatGPT do the demo.

Suppose consumers ask if you have a specific solution. In that case, you can use the AI question answering feature in an elevator pitch format to mention the key features without requiring visitors to read through your complete product information to persuade prospects to leave their information to discuss the application and a short list of the main capabilities. Customers may also ask if a specific feature is involved, in which case you would then reply 'yes' as you mention the capability or include these functions in your product description in case prospects wish to make a self-service evaluation. This 3.5s question can help persuade clients to learn more even if their capabilities are not listed/mentioned explicitly. Furthermore, you can add conversation links to your competitive detail so that users can examine public negative data about rivals or add general industry issues or threats that your solution can deal with, to persuade clients that they are in the correct spot. Typically, a notice of "0.5s" of the business name isn't present, but it would take more than 5s for you to add your company's approach of dealing with certain topics/threats.

CHAPTER 6

ChatGPT for Marketing Strategies

Understand why customers' problems are important - By posing the prompt "What actions or activities do you take to avoid issue X?" marketers can learn why a customer's problem is important to them. When faced with a challenge, humans respond with an action - they avoid the challenge entirely through inaction, or they respond with activities aimed at overcoming the barrier. By asking individuals about their strategies, we infer the severity of a problem. In our work looking at social chat data for a mental health services NLP center, we found that the magnitude of impact on an individual is better expressed by the time intensity of avoidant strategies, while financial avoidance activities are a more universal sign of a problem. Understanding impacts helps inform value propositions to customers. If a brand makes it clear that its product can minimize the disruption in the customers' lives, loyalty may increase. Costs of a problem represent a target for return-on-investment (ROI) claims that are often featured in marketing collateral and proofs of sales.

The following three sections address more tactical use-cases that have the potential to impact the messaging and design of how businesses create brand and value propositions to their customer segments. First, we discuss how a customer's open-ended description of a problem helps marketers determine why the problem is important to solve. Next, we discuss how automation of the design thinking process becomes possible with ChatGPT, a capability that we use to supplement ethnographic insights into a customer segment to fuel ideation and brainstorming for concepts that align with unmet customer needs and important problems to solve. Finally, we guide you through a modeling technique to help brand managers recognize how changes made to a product during product development should be reflected in a new or evolving value proposition to help increase the potential for commercial success.

CHAPTER 7

ChatGPT for Customer Support

A fine-tuned model like ChatGPT can bring an efficiency improvement. The efficiency can be measured by many factors, such as the higher acceptance rate or higher purchase rates. Several strategies can help contribute to higher efficiency. One possible example is to limit chat replies. ChatGPT can give longer replies than domain-oriented chatbots and have a tenuous workflow. Furthermore, the model cannot truly filter out sensitive information, thus giving generic and meticulous responses. A response could also tend to be generic and at times irrelevant. A limited chat reply would transfer a conversation back to the human agent or customer service representative (CSR) and avoid unwanted back-and-forth responses or irrelevant conversations. Improved acceptance rates can be achieved with a fine-tuned ChatGPT by providing the best HR or CSR assistance. Banned words can be avoided and a supervised fine-tuned chatbot can recommend or reply with the best response.

Running a chatbot for customer support can be set up within minutes at much smaller costs. However, it is important to realize that the drawbacks of running a chatbot for chat use cases are tangible. For instance, following up on a customer's query might be more complicated than a text-only chatbot that only needs to interact with a single server (e.g., shopping or flight booking chatbots). It is commonplace for humans still to deal with returned faulty items and requests for refunds or exchanges. This could easily be done by a chatbot that responds within a minute for middle to high-level language proficiency. Customers could then anticipate quick resolution (or not), which could lead to a faster acceptance rate. Moreover, a satisfied customer would more likely return to the ecommerce site even if the costs of running a server to maintain the chatbot are significant. The most significant improvement is customer purchases and reconnect with the service.

CHAPTER 8

Ensuring Data Privacy and Security

It is widely recognized that in order to produce decent quality interactions, chatbots need to have been properly trained. This usually involves large amounts of data, which is typically used as a supervised training set. The conversation interface neo also needs to be formalized. Of course, the resulting system stores that information in a way that is somehow encoded in its machine learning algorithms. As the popularity of proposed transformers architectures has already made it clear to everyone, these models are already as sensitive to biases in the training data and the choice of response hyperparameters. In certain cases of fine-tuning, the initial knowledge can be a limiting factor. In addition, the response generation process is typically probabilistic, so there is always some uncertainty when approaching chatbot responses as a quick description of the system. High temperature and nucleus sampling techniques serve as rough heuristics to widen the output possibilities and encourage a bit of creativity, and these solutions are essential for avoiding repetitive and stereotyped responses.

It's very important to be careful about any sensitive data that you are providing in the prompt for ChatGPT. Dataguard also offers custom NLP for you to train a GPT model using your sensitive data, preventing ChatGPT from ever seeing or interacting with it. We also offer secure support for chat conversations that is designed to protect your data from any breach, which is very important. Another option is to do a sanity check of the data to ensure that you, the user, are not sharing anything sensitive, and use obscure references like "upcoming project" instead of something mission-critical.

CHAPTER 9

Training and Managing ChatGPT

GPT-2 was trained on a multiway classification task, allowing it to provide answers to specific input prompts. Training examples consist of an input prompt and a task label associated with the correct output response. The input prompt can be, for example, a bit of text to be summarized, a question to be answered, or a statement that the model should complete. The training objective for each input prompt then requires a high classification score—close to 1—for the correct task label, while disfavored task labels are assigned an exponentially-weighted lower probability. Each task label corresponds to a possible output response that the model should produce given the input prompt. The output can then be generated by initiating inference from the desired output and conducting a top-k sampling.

Figure 9: Use of data to train fine-tuned models. Fine-tuning a model requires task-specific training data relevant to the domain. The fine-tuned model, specific to a certain domain, can be further trained with data from the same domain or with the global ChatGPT model. Domain-specific fine-tuning can be repeated iteratively using more data, resulting in performance improvements. Alternatively, training a domain-specific model further with global data will result in a deeper understanding of the global commonsense knowledge.

Figure 8: Conceptual framework for training an AI model to perform a task. ChatGPT was trained on conversations in order to learn how to have conversation-like interactions (top path). In the same way, a language model can be trained from exemplar conversations alone (bottom path). This model can then be fine-tuned on a limited set of task-specific dialogues so as to be able to perform tasks.

CHAPTER 10

Monitoring and Improving Performance

Look for confusion. One of the biggest issues with the NLP system is the fusion of verbiage (different phases) mentioned to call an action. When verbiage is identical in intent, the NLP system has an easier time recognizing intent and taking the action based on that intent. If competing verbiage phases exist which are associated with different intents, the NLP system can struggle to make the correct decision as to the required intent of the user action. Review transcripts to understand the full verbiage that is used for the same end result and identify which results are difficult for the model to properly recognize.

Analyze spellings, slang, and vernacular usage. In an end-to-end model, there is no "Spell Check" and it's important to understand the different possible spellings. Sometimes, what the user has said ('slang') will be in input and you'll need to remove it before analysis. There are multiple parameters for a determination of a 'spell'. These include spell check of words, public dictionary of washdowns, spell check of vassal unicode, etc. Remember to keep in mind the source from which the verbiage comes (Market, Industry, regent, etc.) when doing this and apply these conditions before doing spell check.

Turn logging on. Do not track user requests. Log at least the expressions closest to actions executed by the Contact Center agent or the closest expression asked. For instance, if the user asked for "list of banks" and the agent answered "chase bank", the transcription can be "list of banks. Chase bank" or something similar. Do not log sensitive information such as social security numbers, phone numbers, credit card numbers, etc. Do not track requests that are not followed up by the agent. (This means look only at user to agent interactions for Performance Analysis).

Continuous tracking of the model to track any performance change is very important to ensure that it is providing good responses and is not saying anything unwanted. Here is how you can monitor and analyze the performance of the model. Feel free to use the provided scripts to perform analysis.

CHAPTER 11

Integrating ChatGPT with Existing Systems

In this chapter, you will learn how to make ChatGPT work directly with your everyday systems with minimal to no code. ChatGPT creators have presented APIs and have provided a detailed guide to help non-technical users. At the time of writing this book, they released 15 integrations to many popular systems. Business leaders can now integrate ChatGPT with these systems by dragging and dropping actions from the UI and use ChatGPT capabilities. With the guide, business leaders can also write code in most of the systems to integrate with the API. You can also make ChatGPT work with many systems which have a variety of these APIs by writing code in most of the systems as ChatGPT supports REST APIs. In the chapter, you will learn step by step how to make ChatGPT work with the systems presented in the guide.

As a business leader, you might use many tools and systems to automate business operations and achieve goals. In your organization, you are using internal communication tools, customer relationship management (CRM) systems, project management tools, helpdesk and customer support tools, and custom applications and integrations. You might wonder how to use the output provided by ChatGPT in these systems to get the most out of it. You might also wonder how to make

ChatGPT work directly from these systems, so that the chat history and responses from ChatGPT are stored in your systems.

CHAPTER 12

Scaling ChatGPT for Large Businesses

Closing Notes: While detailed examples in the paper presented several minor extensions to the ChatGPT platform, I see this project as modular and easily extensible in general. Many improvements are applicable for any conversational workflow. The goal is not only to democratize access to models but to provide an API and platform that enables businesses to comfortably drive ChatGPT to its full potential. We look forward to developing software for clients triumphantly, adding new platforms and providers, and beginning more conversations about ChatGPT implementation and challenges ranging from conversational flows in games to multimodal conversation training. Finally, this project also opens a multitude of new conversation AI research opportunities. Transitioning from model research to end-use applications extends the domain of potential insights from dialog agents. More challenges and novel and industry-generic architectures are described in the following guidelines when building scalable dialog architectures, generic implementation designs, and rigorous testing and deployment pipelines.

There's a category of enterprise use cases tailored for ChatGPT, which includes legal, HR, IT, and marketing support. Many other use cases might already have existing domain-specific data sources to train specific domain-savvy models, but ChatGPT can still be applicable as a backup when there is no good data, or as a complement to handle low confidence scenarios. This is known as "DialoGPT - a persona-based model trained on some persona-defined dialogs" usage. To avoid catching ourselves on a chatbot hammer, which will stop being able to solve every problem like it is a nail, the detailed analysis of successful use cases is beneficial. Then we can introduce more complex flows around models that enhance the service. This approach is likely to thrive in the patterns of conversation 2.0.

Businesses often use more than chat to serve clients. Hence, scaling ChatGPT involves making it extensible and data-driven, adding role-based interaction, integrating with cloud solutions, and securing it. The following are some tips from this approach that could be useful for those at larger businesses applying ChatGPT and also technical conversational AI enthusiasts.

CHAPTER 13

Overcoming Challenges and Limitations

Natural language models are far from perfect and do not accurately represent the real world. There are pitfalls in excesses such as inconsistency, bias, politicization, and immorality. People are flawed, and therefore models created from people are also flawed. Like people, these models are never neutral or safe. They can be biased, oppressive, and capable of causing harm. The use of such models in production must be cautious. Common-sense knowledge can be harmful when flawed humans overflow into the flawed AI model. Data poisoning and AI algorithms that are dedicated to increasing human mistrust and divisiveness can separate large communities. Understanding the limits of such models is important. It is not widely known how dangerous these neural networks can be. We must understand their limits to build an AI safeguard against malicious use of this increasingly sophisticated technology.

ChatGPT is a game-changing technology, but there are some challenges and limitations in fully achieving its potential. In the next few years, these may be mitigated or solved entirely as the technology continues to evolve. However, in the short-term, readers should be aware of what limitations come with the technology in its current form and have a strategy for working within these limitations. Although AI is progressing rapidly, additional research, discovery, and innovation is needed to improve business applications of ChatGPT. Over the next several years, significant challenges may be overcome, such as transforming ChatGPT into an entirely unsupervised learning model.

CHAPTER 14

Ethical Considerations with ChatGPT

Unfortunately, as of yet, GPT models have developed quite a strong potential for niche capabilities. But here are some of the general guidelines that we could still focus on in future chat-based models. During usage, the individual gen z pundits could consider the following guidelines for crop models and their development. EntityType models should principally respect individuals, emotions, gender identity, and pronouns. Models should not have a negative influence on people. Models should be gender expansive. Providing personal advice on attempting to promote support is not advised. Data-bound relationships cannot be classified as true therapeutic interactions. Models cannot replace mentors or guardians. Handle sensitive queries by encouraging professional support. Always preface with a cautionary disclaimer about expert financial or medical advice. Proceed with these other lenses and please consult professionals. Should be finally revered to ensure yielding results.

Models that implore the transformation of distinct characteristics should always be developed with sensitivity towards the implications for engaging with that characteristic and potentially misrepresent it. The benefits would be transformed to generate altruism and empathy, generate inclusion and connect in the midst of diversity. Social proximity generated could potentiate potential relationships and reduce prejudice and bullying. Creation of shared language will facilitate group work. If GPT models were trained to avoid stereotyping and overt in-group favoritism, they could also encourage mindful, deliberate, and respectful interaction between intergroup participants. Models that promote only unique characteristics are more likely to truly resonate and perplex individuals. Models that shy away from controversy and conflict may help model healthy responses for several types of interpersonal interaction.

Now, let's discuss ethical considerations. If you are deploying a system which simulates human-like interaction, there are many risks and ethical questions. The questions can range from what the assistive bots are allowed to say to are they even good for the users? There are systems which allow for powerful language model use, but dialog models can also be fine-tuned to discourage negative, destructive, or risky content. We should strive for models that embody the best of what humans can be, which consists of more than just authenticity, creativity, empathy, humor, and constructive feedback. Our chat bot should also help users to make and maintain positive friendships, help users maintain a positive emotional space, and uphold privacy and emotional boundaries.

CHAPTER 15

Future Trends and Developments

There is a significant gap in performance across conversational agents, and currently research and effort is required to build a system that performs at the capability threshold of state-of-the-art conversational models. Anyone can synthesize a video, but to synthesize a video where an actor plays a young version of themselves, moving, talking, and acting in a way that doesn't flicker or look strange is challenging. A conversational agent exhibits the idea of the uncanny valley where small errors can be jarring, and the user can tell something is off. As Tariq of unique.ai discussed with me, "traditional machine learning developers focus mostly on services because of a lack of data and ambition in using deeper learning methods. Enterprises are now more so obliged to find an AI partner or hire an NLP/NLU expert to use modern AI models effectively in conversations."

A report by EY reports that only 13% of businesses have a full suite of conversational AI that covers different use cases within their organization. This lag is, in part, because developing a successful conversational AI solution is no small feat. For conversational agents to engage humans fluidly in dialogue, they must master two areas where the dominant AI systems trained through supervised learning struggle.

The explosion of chatbots and conversational AI has been driven by the booming business potential of the conversational channel. As a result, over 47% of companies worldwide are currently investing to raise the overall intelligence of their chatbot solutions. Whilst tools have made it easier than ever to experiment with new ideas, there is a misunderstanding that platforms on their own can do all the work. The problem with off-the-shelf AI is that they need a lot of customization to seem real (or, at the very least, useful) and businesses often lack the expertise in language processing to bridge the gap.

CHAPTER 16

Conclusion

Like other tools of similar nature, GPT-3 has its weak points. Companies that are hoping to entirely depend on it will become frustrated if they do not understand these points. However, this does not mean that the tool is unhelpful. Business owners must first find out how to extract the most value from OpenAI's GPT-3 in a way that complies with social and ethical responsibility. After they have done that, the only thing that any company can do is do its best, and execute its plan.

Business owners in just about every kind of industry can benefit from using OpenAI's ChatGPT, as long as they understand what it can and cannot do. While the GPT-3 language model has its limitations, businesses can leverage it to boost the bottom line and rise above the competition. Once companies have subscribed to or purchased a license for GPT-3, it will be critical for business owners to familiarize themselves with OpenAI's ethical guidelines and follow their advice to protect both the public and their businesses.